World Beneath the Waves

BY JOY BREWSTER

Table of Contents

The Oceans of the World

Almost three-fourths of Earth's surface is covered with oceans. Under these oceans are the tallest mountains and the deepest valleys in the world.

Oceans are important to all living things, even those on land. Oceans provide food and **minerals**. Oceans also influence Earth's climate by moderating temperatures around the globe and providing moisture for rainfall.

The continents divide the ocean into four major regions: the Pacific Ocean, the Atlantic Ocean, the Indian Ocean, and the Arctic Ocean. Although we think of these oceans as separate, they are not; they are all connected and water flows from one to the other.

The equator divides Earth into two **hemispheres**. The Northern Hemisphere is the area above the equator. The Southern Hemisphere is the area below the equator.

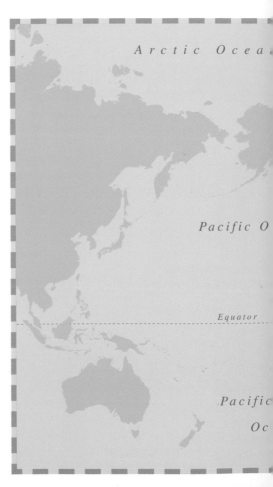

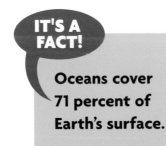

IT'S A FACT!

Oceans cover 71 percent of Earth's surface.

Northern Hemisphere

Equator

Southern Hemisphere

SOLVE THIS!

1 About what percent of Earth's surface is covered by land?

In which hemisphere do oceans cover the largest amount of Earth's surface area?

Arctic Ocean

Atlantic Ocean

Equator

Indian Ocean

THE FOUR OCEANS OF THE WORLD

Ocean	Approximate size (surface area)	Average Depth	Deepest Point	Amazing Facts
Pacific	64 million square miles 165 million square kilometers	14,000 feet 4,282 meters	Mariana Trench 36,000 feet 11,022 meters	This ocean covers one-third of Earth's surface and is larger than all the continents put together.
Atlantic	32 million square miles 82 million square kilometers	12,800 feet 3,926 meters	Puerto Rico Trench 30,100 feet 9,200 meters	An underwater mountain range called the Mid-Atlantic Ridge runs down the middle; this is the largest feature on Earth.
Indian	28 million square miles 73 million square kilometers	13,000 feet 3,963 meters	Java Trench 24,400 feet 7,460 meters	Much of the Indian Ocean lies in the tropics. The smallest fish in the ocean, the goby, lives here. It grows to less than one-half inch long.
Arctic	5 million square miles 13 million square kilometers	3,900 feet 1,205 meters	Eurasia basin 14,100 feet 4,300 meters	This ocean is covered in ice most of the year. The North Pole is near the center of the ocean. The Arctic ice sheet can be as thick as sixty-five feet.

This pie chart shows the percentage of Earth's total ocean surface area each ocean occupies.

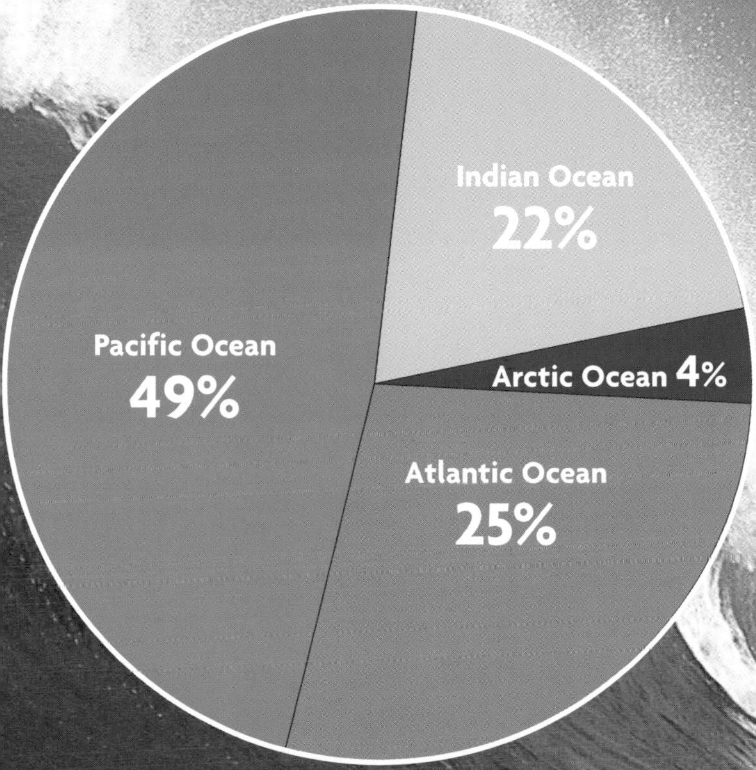

↓

Indian Ocean
22%

Pacific Ocean
49%

Arctic Ocean 4%

Atlantic Ocean
25%

SOLVE THIS!

❷ **Which is the deepest ocean? Which is the shallowest ocean?**

About how many times bigger is the Pacific Ocean than the Arctic Ocean? Than the Atlantic Ocean?

If one mile is 5,280 feet, estimate how deep 12,400 feet is in miles. Is it 4-5 miles? 2-3 miles? 3-4 miles?

TRUE OR FALSE: The larger the ocean, the greater its average depth. Explain your answer.

IT'S A FACT!

The average depth of the oceans is about 10,935 feet, or 3,344 meters.

5

You already know that almost three-fourths of Earth's surface—about seventy-one percent—is covered with ocean water. But did you know that the oceans are so deep and so vast that they hold ninety-seven percent of the world's water? Of the remaining three percent, a little more than two percent is in glaciers and ice caps. That means that less than one percent of the world's water is in rivers, lakes, water vapor in the air, and living things— including you!

THE WORLD'S WATER

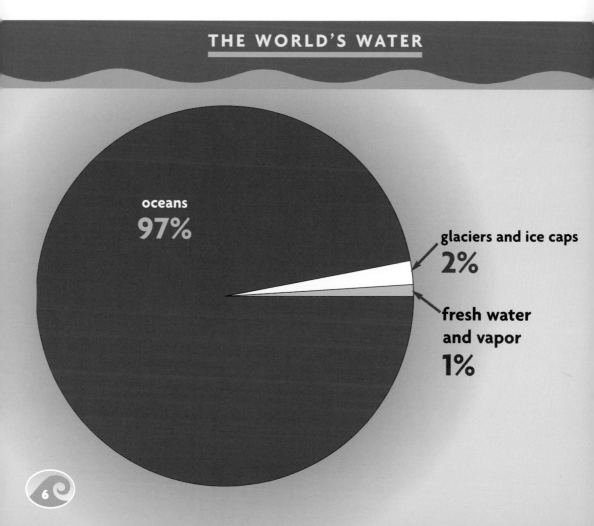

oceans
97%

glaciers and ice caps
2%

fresh water and vapor
1%

SOLVE THIS!

3 Imagine 100 glasses of water representing the world's water. How many would be filled with fresh water? With salt water?

If you collected six gallons of salt water in a bucket and let the water evaporate, how much salt would be left in the bottom of the bucket?

Ocean water is salty because it contains lots of **sodium chloride**, or table salt. This is the same salt you use to flavor your food. The salt in the ocean comes from water that flows over the land in the form of rivers and streams. As the water washes over rocks and soil, it picks up salt and other minerals and carries them into the ocean. This salt dissolves in the ocean, leaving it—well, salty! Each gallon of ocean water contains about two-thirds of a cup of salt.

A gallon of water from the Atlantic Ocean is heavier than a gallon of water from the Pacific Ocean because Atlantic Ocean water has more salt in it. Because of the presence of salt, ocean water freezes at a lower temperature than fresh water.

WHATEVER FLOATS YOUR BOAT

Try this experiment to find out how the properties of salt water are different from the properties of fresh water.

Fill two plastic containers with three cups of fresh water each.

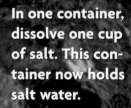

In one container, dissolve one cup of salt. This container now holds salt water.

SOLVE THIS!

❹ If fresh water freezes at 0° Celsius, what's its freezing point in degrees Fahrenheit?

If salt water freezes at about −19° Celsius, what's its freezing point in degrees Fahrenheit?

To convert Celsius to Fahrenheit, multiply the Celsius temperature by ⁹/₅, and then add 32.

Place one egg in the fresh water and one egg in the salt water.

What happens to the egg in each container? How do you think this fact affects marine animals? How does it affect divers?

The Ocean in Motion

The ocean is always moving: **waves** break on the surface, sea levels rise and fall with the **tides**, and **currents** flow below the surface.

Although it looks as if the water in a wave is moving across the surface of the ocean, it is not. The water is actually moving up and down. This is why an object on top of a wave will bob up and down, but not move forward.

When a wave reaches the shore, however, the water does move forward. It surges onto the shore. This is because the "bottom" of the wave drags on the sand and the "top" continues on, crashing onto the shore. This crashing water is called the surf.

Most waves are caused by wind blowing across the ocean's surface. The size of a wave depends on how fast and how far the wind blows over the surface and on the depth of the wave. Small winds can cause ripples, while strong winds create large hurricane waves.

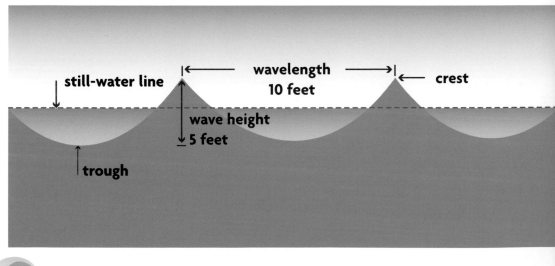

still-water line | wavelength 10 feet | crest

wave height 5 feet

trough

WALLS OF WATER

Large waves caused by under-water volcanoes and earth-quakes are called **tsunamis** (tsoo-NAH-meez). Some people call them tidal waves, but that's not an accurate name because they have nothing to do with the tides. These enormous waves can be 100 feet tall and travel across an ocean. Tsunamis have destroyed entire seaside cities. The largest tsunami ever recorded was in Siberia in 1737. The giant wave reached 210 feet.

The highest part of a wave is called the crest. The lowest part is called the trough (TROF). The **wave height** is the distance between the crest and the trough. The **wavelength** is the distance between a crest and the next crest. The still-water line is the level of the water if there were no waves.

SOLVE THIS!

5 What is the wave height of this wave? What is its wavelength?

Along most shorelines, water levels rise and fall twice a day. These changes, called tides, are caused by the gravitational pull of the Sun and the Moon. The ocean surface lifts, or bulges, in two places: on the side of Earth that faces the Moon and on the side of Earth that faces away from the Moon. Both bulges cause a high tide on nearby shorelines. At the same time that the high tides occur, low tides occur between the two bulges.

← Compare the Bay of Fundy at high tide with the Bay of Fundy at low tide. ↓

Spring tides and neap tides each occur twice a month.
↓

SPRING TIDE   NEAP TIDE

Tides are also affected by the pull of the Sun, although the effect of the Sun is not as great as the effect of the Moon. When the Moon and Sun are lined up with Earth, the combined pull is the strongest, causing the highest high tides and the lowest low tides. These very high and very low tides are called spring tides. Weaker tides, called neap tides, happen when the Moon and the Sun are at right angles to Earth.

High tides alternate with low tides. Along most shorelines, a high tide or low tide occurs about every six hours.

SOLVE THIS!

6 If a high tide occurs at 8:00 a.m., at what time would you expect a low tide? When would you expect the next high tide?

Giant rivers of water, called currents, flow throughout the ocean, transporting water, plants, and animals long distances. Surface currents carry warm water to the poles and cold water to the tropics.

The Gulf Stream in the Atlantic Ocean is an example of a warm-water current. It travels north along the eastern coast of the United States, carrying water from the tropics.

SOLVE THIS!

7 Where is the hottest ocean water?

Where is the coldest ocean water?

How much can ocean temperatures range?

TOO COLD

The average temperature of the ocean is 4° Celsius, but temperatures vary a lot depending on location and ocean depth:

- The average temperature of the water at the surface of the ocean ranges from 30° Celsius in the tropics to -2° Celsius near the poles.

- The deeper you go in the ocean, the colder it gets, but it's not always cold near the ocean floor. In some places, you'll find hot water vents deep in the ocean valleys. The water here can reach 260° Celsius when it bursts out from cracks in the ocean floor, heated by the molten rock beneath Earth's crust.

Arctic O

Pacific Ocean

← This map shows how the major long-distance surface currents flow. Warm-water currents are shown with red arrows, cold-water currents with blue arrows.

Down Under

When you fly over land, you can see canyons, mountains, and plains. You might even see a volcano. When you fly over the ocean, it looks rather flat. But hidden beneath the surface is the ocean floor. This is where you'll find the deepest canyons, the tallest mountains, the longest mountain range, and most of the active volcanoes in the world!

Scientists divide the ocean floor into three main parts: the **continental shelf**, the **continental slope**, and the **deep ocean floor**, or abyss (uh-BISS).

continental shelf
600 feet deep

continental slope
1,200 feet deep

abyssal plain
12,400 feet de

The continental shelf is found around the edges of the world's continents, where the land slopes from the shore into the ocean. The outer edge of this shallow shelf is about 600 feet underwater.

At the edge of a continental shelf, the ocean floor drops steeply. This is the continental slope. The slope reaches depths of about 1,200 feet.

Beyond this point is the deep ocean floor. Most of the deep ocean floor is covered with flat **abyssal plains**. But there are also long mountain ranges called **ocean ridges**. Earthquakes and volcanoes are commonly found at the ocean ridges. Deep valleys called **trenches** are also found along the deep ocean floor.

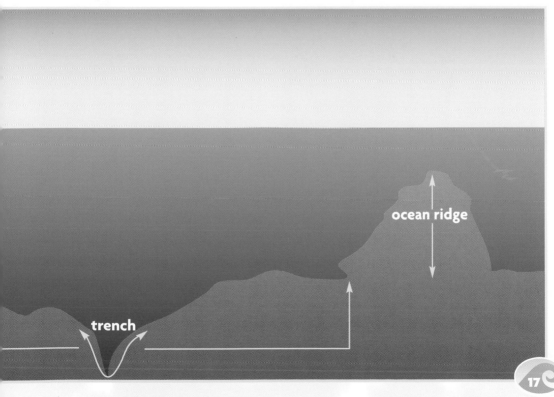

ocean ridge

trench

Compare these underwater valleys and mountains with the most impressive examples on land:

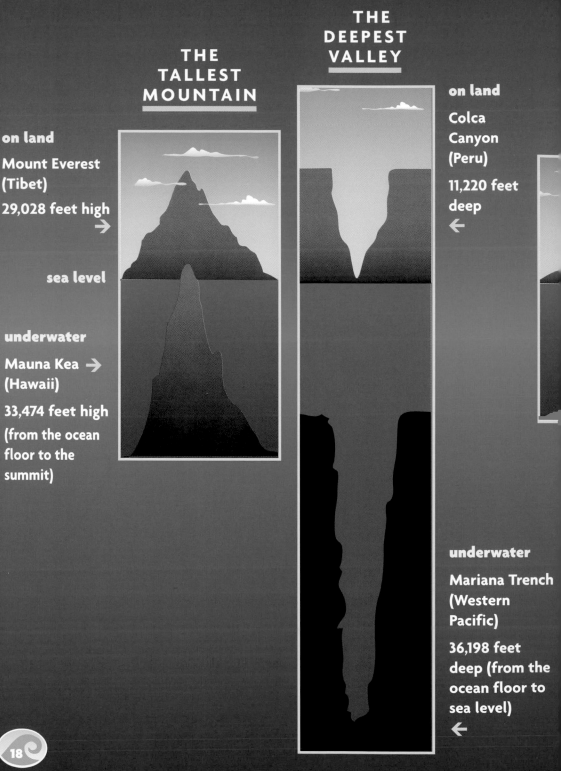

THE TALLEST MOUNTAIN

THE DEEPEST VALLEY

on land

Mount Everest (Tibet)

29,028 feet high →

sea level

underwater

Mauna Kea → (Hawaii)

33,474 feet high (from the ocean floor to the summit)

on land

Colca Canyon (Peru)

11,220 feet deep ←

underwater

Mariana Trench (Western Pacific)

36,198 feet deep (from the ocean floor to sea level) ←

THE LONGEST MOUNTAIN RANGE

on land   Himalayas (Tibet)   4,500 miles long ↓

underwater   Mid-Ocean Ridge   46,000 miles long ↑

HAWAIIAN VOLCANO ISLANDS

Did you know that the islands of Hawaii are actually the tops of volcanoes rising from the ocean floor? These volcanoes first erupted about 25 million years ago — and they're still active today. These islands are known as an archipelago, which is a chain of islands. Volcanoes are erupting under the waves all the time — about 90 percent of all volcanic activity on Earth occurs in the ocean!

SOLVE THIS!

8 If 13,796 feet of Mauna Kea stands above sea level as an island, how deep is the water there?

If one mile is 5,280 feet, how many miles deeper is the Mariana Trench than the Colca Canyon?

Estimate about how many times longer the Mid-Ocean Ridge is than the Himalayas.

The oceans have different levels, or zones. Zones are defined by how far down sunlight penetrates the water. Each zone's light, temperature, and pressure create unique habitats for different animals. The three main zones are the sunlight zone, the twilight zone, and the midnight zone.

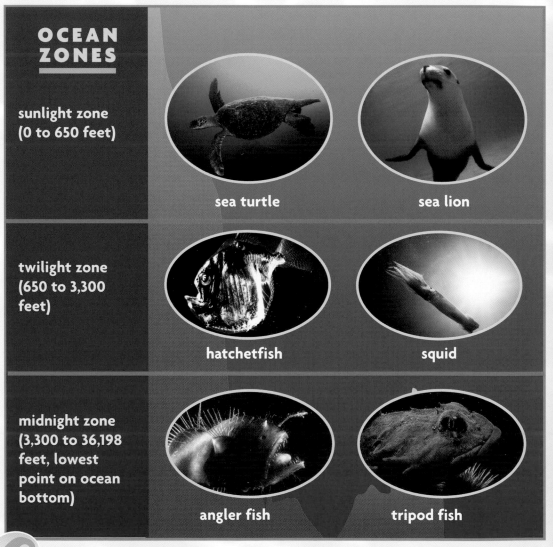

OCEAN ZONES

sunlight zone (0 to 650 feet)

sea turtle

sea lion

twilight zone (650 to 3,300 feet)

hatchetfish

squid

midnight zone (3,300 to 36,198 feet, lowest point on ocean bottom)

angler fish

tripod fish

The sunlight zone: This is the top layer of the ocean, where sunlight penetrates the water. Plants need sunlight to survive, so this is the only zone where you'll find ocean plants such as **phytoplankton** (fye-toh-PLANGK-tuhn) and seaweed. More than ninety percent of all marine life lives here.

The twilight zone: Almost no light can penetrate water at this dark, murky depth. It's too dark for plants to grow here. Only a few smaller animals live here, preying on other animals or eating the dead plants and animals that fall from the sunlight zone. In this dim zone, animals such as squid must detect their prey by vibrations and scent.

The midnight zone: The water pressure here is immense. The only light in these depths comes from animals with built-in "flashlights." Down here you'll find hot water vents—cracks in the ocean floor that shoot out incredibly hot water filled with minerals. Bacteria thrive on the heat and minerals, providing a food source for deep-sea animals.

SOLVE THIS!

9 The Empire State Building is 1,250 feet tall. The Washington Monument is 555 feet tall. If these colossal structures were placed underwater so that their tops touched the surface, which zones would they reach?

What's the largest zone of the ocean? Is that where most of the animals live?

SOLVE THIS!

10 How much pressure is pushing on something 3,000 meters deep in the ocean?
If one atmosphere equals 15 pounds of pressure, how many pounds of pressure would you feel at a depth of 300 meters?

Believe it or not, scientists have explored only one percent of the world's oceans. Underwater exploration is difficult in this vast, dark, and cold environment. The main problem is the incredible pressure—which can be 16,000 pounds per square inch in the deepest trenches. That's like having the weight of an entire elephant on your toe!

Despite these challenges, scientists have studied all the different underwater areas, from the sunlight zone to the ocean trenches.

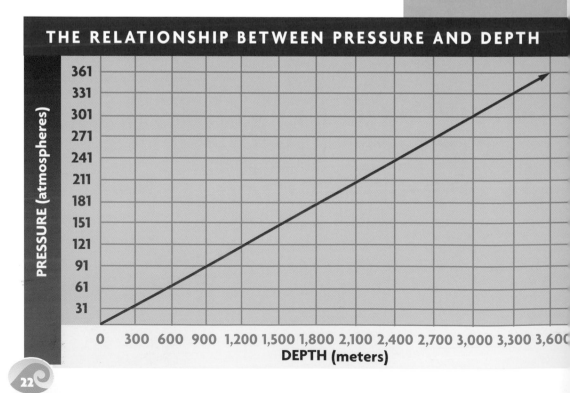

THE RELATIONSHIP BETWEEN PRESSURE AND DEPTH

PRESSURE (atmospheres): 361, 331, 301, 271, 241, 211, 181, 151, 121, 91, 61, 31

DEPTH (meters): 0, 300, 600, 900, 1,200, 1,500, 1,800, 2,100, 2,400, 2,700, 3,000, 3,300, 3,600

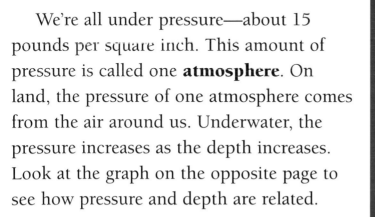

We're all under pressure—about 15 pounds per square inch. This amount of pressure is called one **atmosphere**. On land, the pressure of one atmosphere comes from the air around us. Underwater, the pressure increases as the depth increases. Look at the graph on the opposite page to see how pressure and depth are related.

It's easy to see why divers can't go more than a few hundred feet deep—even with scuba (air) gear to help them breathe. A few hundred feet below the surface, the pressure is so great it would crush a diver's body. Even with a pressurized suit, divers can reach depths of only 1,500 feet.

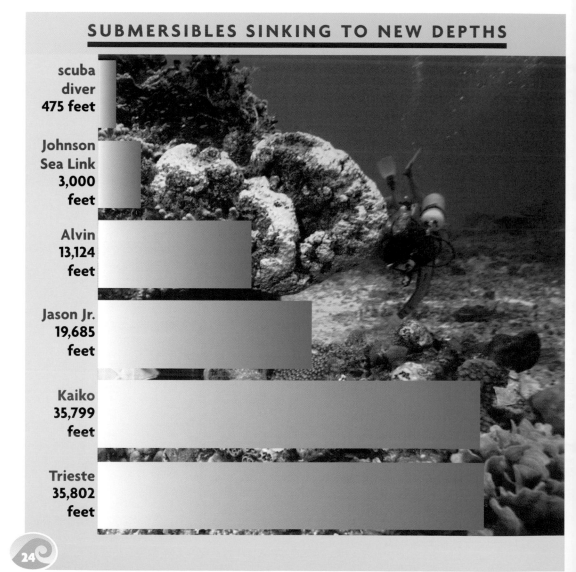

SUBMERSIBLES SINKING TO NEW DEPTHS

scuba
diver
475 feet

Johnson
Sea Link
**3,000
feet**

Alvin
**13,124
feet**

Jason Jr.
**19,685
feet**

Kaiko
**35,799
feet**

Trieste
**35,802
feet**

SOLVE THIS!

Special vehicles known as **submersibles** are needed to go deeper than 1,500 feet. These vehicles are designed to withstand pressures in different ocean depths.

There are different kinds of submersibles:

• Manned submersibles, such as *Alvin*, *Johnson Sea Link*, and *Trieste*, carry a human crew.

• Remotely operated vehicles (ROVs), such as *Kaiko* and *Jason Jr.*, don't carry people. Scientists use cameras and computers to operate ROVs from manned submarines.

11 *Shinkai* is a three-passenger Japanese submersible. If it can dive 8,290 feet deeper than *Alvin*, how deep can it descend?

Scientists often use submersibles to explore shipwrecks on the ocean floor. One of the most famous shipwrecks is the *Titanic*. This "unsinkable" ship sank in 1912. About 1,500 men, women, and children lost their lives.

In 1985, Dr. Robert Ballard and a team of researchers found the remains of the *Titanic* in the Atlantic off the coast of Newfoundland.

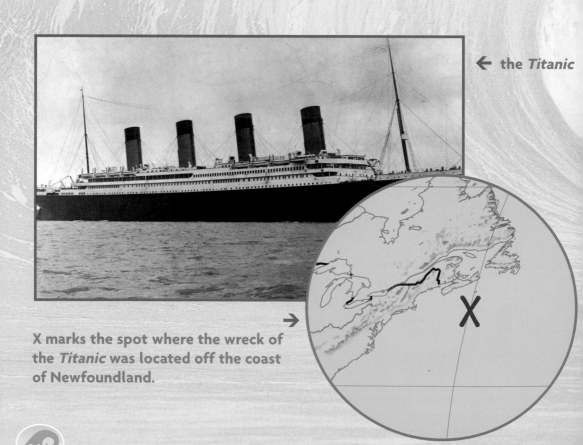

← the *Titanic*

→ X marks the spot where the wreck of the *Titanic* was located off the coast of Newfoundland.

Dr. Ballard and his team used the submersible *Alvin* to explore the wreck of the *Titanic* a year later. It took them two and a half hours to descend to the wreck, which was resting at a depth of 13,000 feet.

From inside *Alvin*, the team operated the unmanned robot *Jason Jr.* as it explored the remains of the *Titanic*. By using both kinds of submersibles, Dr. Ballard and his team were able to observe that some things looked almost as good as new, even after spending seventy-five years on the ocean floor.

↑ *Jason Jr.* before the *Titanic* expedition

← This bag and its contents belonged to a ship's officer on the *Titanic*.

The Never-Ending Adventure

Submersibles give us a close-up look at the ocean floor, but how do scientists measure ocean depths, identify mountain ranges, and find deep-sea trenches?

In the early days, sailors measured ocean depths by lowering weights tied to a long piece of rope into the water. The depth was measured by noting how much of the rope was in the water when the weight hit the bottom.

Today, scientists are able to get a much better sense of what lies beneath the surface of the oceans. One technique they use is sonar. Sound waves are "bounced" off the ocean floor, and the time it takes them to return is measured.

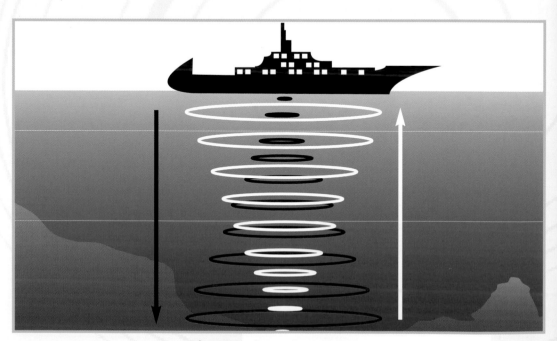

↑ This ship is bouncing sonar waves off the ocean floor to learn about its features.

This is what the ocean floor looks like from a satellite.

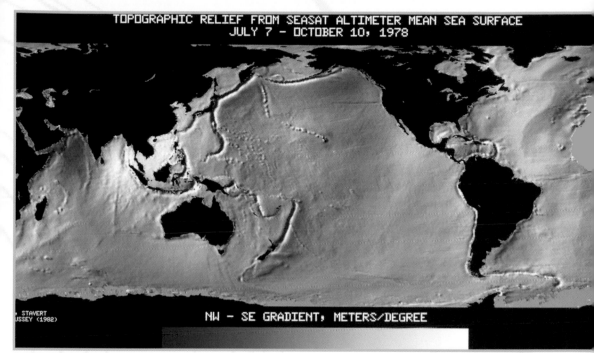

TOPOGRAPHIC RELIEF FROM SEASAT ALTIMETER MEAN SEA SURFACE
JULY 7 - OCTOBER 10, 1978

STAVERT
USSEY (1982)

NW - SE GRADIENT, METERS/DEGREE

Another way scientists study the ocean floor is from space. Just as ships use sound waves, satellites circling Earth bounce microwaves off the ocean floor. These readings give a much more detailed picture of the oceans' geography, from subtle hills and valleys to hidden trenches.

Even with this modern technology, scientists have only just started to uncover the secrets of the oceans. There are many more trenches to investigate, marine species to discover, and mysteries of the oceans' power to solve. Many exciting discoveries are ahead as we explore Earth's watery frontier!

CHAPTER 1

Solve This! Answers

1 Page 3
29 percent; Southern Hemisphere

2 Page 5
Pacific; Arctic; about 12 times; about 2 times; 2-3 miles; False; the Atlantic Ocean is larger than the Indian Ocean, but the Indian Ocean has a greater average depth.

3 Page 7
1; 97; 4 cups

4 Page 9
32° Fahrenheit; −2.2° Fahrenheit

5 Page 11
5 feet; 10 feet

6 Page 13
2:00 p.m.; 8:00 p.m.

7 Page 15
Near the hot-water vents; near the poles; 262° Celsius

8 Page 19
19,678 feet; 4.7 miles; about 10 times longer

9 Page 21
Empire State Building: twilight zone; Washington Monument: sunlight zone; midnight zone; no, most animals live in the sunlight zone

10 Page 22
301 atmospheres; 465 pounds

11 Page 25
21,414 feet

Glossary

abyssal plains	vast flat or gently sloping regions of the *deep ocean floor*
atmosphere	unit used to measure air or water pressure; one atmosphere equals 15 pounds of pressure
continental shelf	the underwater ledge that stretches from the edge of a continent or island to the *continental slope*
continental slope	the steep drop from the *continental shelf* to the ocean floor
current	water that moves long distances through the ocean
deep ocean floor	the vast area of the ocean bottom; it includes plains, mountains, and valleys
hemisphere	one half of Earth; the Northern and Southern Hemispheres are divided by the equator
minerals	chemical substances found in nature that are neither animal nor plant
ocean ridge	long mountain range along the ocean floor; often the site of earthquakes and volcanoes
phytoplankton	ocean plants that live in the sunlight zone
sodium chloride	salt
submersible	a vehicle used to explore the ocean depths
tide	the rise and fall in the ocean's water level around the world
trench	a long, steep, narrow valley in the ocean floor
tsunami	a very large wave caused by an earthquake or an underwater volcanic eruption
wave	a moving ridge or swell on the surface of the water
wave height	the distance between the crest (highest point) and the trough (lowest point) of a *wave*
wavelength	the distance between two consecutive crests of a *wave*

Index